# It Seems to Me

Stories and Meditations Saying "YES!" to Jesus

*My Life in Words and Actions*

## R. Lynn Sauls

**TEACH Services, Inc.**
P U B L I S H I N G
www.TEACHServices.com • (800) 367-1844

Copyright ©2021

Paintings: "Lynn Meditating at the Edge of Long Pond" and "Mallards Flying over a Beaver Lodge," Roger Blum, Copyright ©2021 by R. Lynn Sauls

World rights reserved. This book or any portion thereof may not be copied or reproduced in any form or manner whatever, except as provided by law, without the written permission of the publisher, except by a reviewer who may quote brief passages in a review.

The author assumes full responsibility for the accuracy of all facts and quotations as cited in this book. The opinions expressed in this book are the author's personal views and interpretations, and do not necessarily reflect those of the publisher.

This book is provided with the understanding that the publisher is not engaged in giving spiritual, legal, medical, or other professional advice. If authoritative advice is needed, the reader should seek the counsel of a competent professional.

---

Copyright © 2021 R. Lynn Sauls
Copyright © 2021 TEACH Services, Inc.
ISBN-13: 978-1-4796-1382-3 (Paperback)
ISBN-13: 978-1-4796-1383-0 (ePub)
Library of Congress Control Number: 2021904253

Unless otherwise noted, all Scriptures are from the King James Version, public domain.

NEB indicates Scripture quotations taken from the New English Bible, copyright © Cambridge University Press and Oxford University Press 1961, 1970. All rights reserved.

NIV indicates THE HOLY BIBLE, NEW INTERNATIONAL VERSION®. Copyright © 1973, 1978, 1984 by International Bible Society. All rights reserved.

NKJV indicates scripture taken from the New King James Version®. Copyright © 1982 by Thomas Nelson. Used by permission. All rights reserved.

Phi indicates The New Testament in Modern English by J.B Phillips copyright © 1960, 1972 J. B. Phillips. Administered by The Archbishops' Council of the Church of England. Used by Permission.

RSV indicates scripture taken from the Revised Standard Version of the Bible, copyright © 1946, 1952, and 1971 the Division of Christian Education of the National Council of the Churches of Christ in the United States of America. Used by permission. All rights reserved.

Jerusalem Bible, Copyright © 1966, 1967 and 1968 by Darton, Longman & Todd Ltd and Doubleday & Company, Inc.

All italics and words in parentheses within quotations are added by the author.

# *Table of Contents*

| | |
|---|---|
| Dedication | v |
| Foreword | vii |
| Acknowledgements | ix |
| Selected Responses To Previously Published Articles | x |
| A Time for Certainty | 11 |
| At the Edge of Restraint | 14 |
| What Katie Rivenbark Taught Us about Witnessing | 17 |
| Company's Coming | 20 |
| Hurricane Preparation | 23 |
| N/A | 26 |
| Friends | 29 |
| Jesus and Journalists | 32 |
| Grapefruit, Ice, and Oxygen | 35 |
| Through a Glass Darkly | 37 |
| Angels | 40 |
| You Never Know — That Child Might Grow Up to Be a Heart Surgeon | 43 |
| Longevity | 46 |
| Throw It into the Garbage Can | 49 |
| Christmas Is for All | 52 |
| Country Roads | 55 |
| Christian Meditation 101 | 57 |
| Meditation on Green | 60 |
| Meditation on Orange | 62 |
| Meditation on Blue | 64 |

Worship and the Fine Arts ........................................................................ 66
Situation for Delight .................................................................................. 71
The Freeing of Long Pond ........................................................................ 75
About the Author ....................................................................................... 81
Bibliography .............................................................................................. 82

# *Dedication*

Dedicated to my wife, Helen Esther Sauls, who recently fell asleep in Jesus after serving Him with me for sixty-seven years. Good memories. A good future when Jesus comes. A good now, knowing Jesus is with me. Every day I sing, "In the morning, when I rise, Give me Jesus. You can have all this world, But give me Jesus."

This book was put together for my former students, colleagues and fans, neighbors and friends, residents and staff of The Gables of Fitchburg, readers who want to know more about Jesus, and especially for members of my dear family. God, who invented free will, doesn't want me to try to convert any of you. That's the work of the Holy Spirit. I just want you to know a little more about Jesus and a man who loves Him and each one of you.

# *Foreword*

### Andy Nash Talks About Lynn Sauls and His Book

In the 1990s, Dr. Sauls was my journalism professor. He once started class with a worship talk. "Today, I will read from Genesis 1," he said. "It was good. It was good. It was very good." Dr. Sauls looked up with a smile. "We were made in God's image. When we create something, we want to be able to say, 'It is good. It is very good.'"

In the 2000s, Lynn was my friend. I was grappling with hard questions about religion, about life. Lynn met me regularly for lunch, gently guiding me. By the end of the decade, I had become a pastor.

In the 2010s, he and Helen had moved back to the northeast to be closer to their son.

Then in August 2020, I heard from Lynn once again. "Andy," he said, "I'm working on two books. My first book will be about …"

I smiled. This was the same man I had loved through the decades. Still living life in all its fullness.

I savored every page of his book—the one you hold in your hands. In this beautiful book filled with memories and insights, Lynn will also be your professor and friend as you travel with him through the decades. Enjoy the journey.

# *Acknowledgements*

The first fifteen articles were selected from a column *Adventist Review* editor William G. Johnsson asked me to write. The series was entitled "It Seems to Me." The others are meditations I had written for *Insight* and the *Review*. I gave all published articles minor or major editing. It was a pleasure working with Donald John, former editor of *Insight*, and Stephen Chavez, associate editor of the *Review*. "Meditation 101," originally given for vespers at the Naples, Florida, Adventist Church is also included.

Here are references for the column articles and the meditations selected:

R. Lynn Sauls, fifteen story articles were selected from the monthly column "It Seems to Me," *Adventist Review*, July 16, 1998, to December 21, 1999.

R. Lynn Sauls, "Meditation on Colors," *Insight*, October 12, 1982, pp. 7–9.

R. Lynn Sauls, "Worship and the Fine Arts," *Adventist Review*, July 5, 1984, pp. 3–4.

Lynn Sauls, "Country Roads," *Insight*, March 14, 1972, pp. 22–23.

Lynn Sauls, "Christian Meditation 101," Presented for vespers at Naples, Florida, Adventist Church, September 11, 1999.

Lynn Sauls, "Situation for Delight," *Insight*, May 2, 1978, pp. 4–6.

Lynn Sauls, "The Freeing of Long Pond," *Insight*, March 29, 1977, pp. 4–9.

# Selected Responses To Previously Published Articles

"Loveliest piece of writing I have encountered."

—Gladyne L. Flether, Wenden, Arizona

"Stimulated my imagination to seek more creative and meaningful ways to spend the Sabbath."

—Janet Bungard, Angwin, California

"You have blessed our readers and helped advance God's work on earth."

—William G. Johnsson, former editor of *Adventist Review*

"Found your articles thoughtful and attractive to all ages. How about submitting some of your articles to a publisher as inspirational messages for many to read and share as gifts to friends?"

—Peggy Kroncke, former vice president for student affairs at Andrews University

*"Well, Peggy, here's the book you called for. Enjoy."*

*—Lynn Sauls*

# *A Time for Certainty*

*I knelt before God
and heard His still,
small voice.*

I was a Christian Scientist in my last year of high school. Carlisle Meacham was a new neighbor who had recently graduated from Atlantic Union College. He was selling Bibles and a book called The Desire of Ages to pay his way at the seminary come fall. I enjoyed talking with him in the evenings. He always listened attentively.

"How could there be evil in the universe?" I questioned. "God is light. When you switch on the light, where does the darkness go? Sin and death are but an illusion."

"Yes," said Carlisle, "when you switch on the light, the darkness seems to end, but it seems to me that you have to account for the shadows."

Carlisle reminded me of what I had learned about Benjamin Franklin in English and history classes.

Franklin discovered electricity, invented bifocals, founded the first American subscription library, and taught Americans how to be healthy, wealthy, and wise through the 10,000 maxims of his *Poor Richard's Almanac*.

But Franklin's greatest legacy was given in 1787 when he was eighty-one years old. The Constitutional Convention was in session in Philadelphia. He listened as the delegates from the thirteen states debated what seemed to be irreconcilable differences. Finally, the time came for him to speak. "Gentlemen, it appears to me …," he began. Too weak to give his speech, he had delegate James Wilson read it for him. It called for compromise between the large states and the small ones. His motion for unanimous consent was carried.

His *Autobiography* tells how he developed the habit of expressing himself in "terms of modest diffidence," never using "the words 'certainly,' 'undoubtedly,' or any others that give the air of positiveness." He felt that this habit was the main reason he was successful in persuading others to accept measures he had been engaged in promoting.[1]

That was the way Carlisle approached me all summer. Then came a change the night before he was scheduled to catch a Greyhound bus that would take him to the seminary.

> *Home alone on New Year's Eve, I knelt before God and heard His still small voice telling me to take the Bible for what it says.*

"Lynn, turn to John 14:2," he said, and he read Jesus' promise to His disciples: "'In my Father's house are many mansions: if it were not so, I would have told you.' Lynn, why don't you accept the Bible for what it says? Why do you spiritualize the meaning away?"

He had me turn to texts about the resurrection, about Jesus showing His scarred hands and side to the disciples, about Jesus letting Thomas touch those scars, about Jesus preparing a meal for His disciples and dining with them early one morning at the Sea of Galilee.

Carlisle finished by having me turn to the story of Jesus' ascension in Acts 1. He read the angels' words to the disciples: "Ye men of Galilee, why stand ye gazing up into heaven? this same Jesus, which is taken up from you into heaven, shall so come in like manner as ye have seen him go into heaven" (verse 11).

---

[1] Benjamin Franklin, *Autobiography of Benjamin Franklin*, ed. John Bigelow, (Philadelphia, J. B. Lippincott & Co., 1868), pp. 228–230.

Carlisle continued, "This was a real Jesus, who suffered a real crucifixion and died a real death. A real body was raised. He could be seen, touched, heard, spoken to. This real Jesus shall come again in the same manner they saw Him go into heaven. Why don't you accept the Bible for what it says? Why do you spiritualize the meaning away?"

Home alone on New Year's Eve, I knelt before God and heard His still small voice telling me to take the Bible for what it says. By spring, I was attending an Adventist church, preparing for baptism, and planning to attend Southern Missionary College (now Southern Adventist University). Thank you, Carlisle Meacham.

There is a place for certainty. But if at first there had been no "It Seems to Me," the certainty would never have gotten through.

So it seems to me.

# *At the Edge of Restraint*

*All the lights are
green—if we go
the right speed.*

It's Monday morning and time to make my weekly commute from Naples, Florida, to Andrews University. I head for Southwest Florida Regional Airport earlier than usual. A storm is forecast to hit by midday. Instead of making a delay on my 12:50 flight, I'll be on standby for the 11:15 and try to get away before the storm hits.

Onto I-75 going north. In the passing lane. Going seventy-five miles an hour—five miles over the limit. Seventy-five on I-75. Troopers won't bother you if you're within five miles over. So I've heard. Passing a number of trucks and cars. Moving right along. Maybe I'll be the first standby and make the 11:15.

From the rearview mirror, I see a Dodge Viper rapidly gaining on me. Tailgating me now. Slowing down. Impatient at my being in the way.

What's wrong with that guy? I'm going five miles over the limit, and still, he wants to pass?

OK, OK! I move over to the regular lane so the speed demon can pass. OK, now pass, you_____(an unflattering word I heard my father use when I was a boy goes through my mind). The Dodge overtakes me as my anger overcomes me. I catch myself going faster. Now eighty miles an hour. Bad thoughts and bad names are directed to the driver of the Dodge, words not used in polite society, words I never use aloud, words that for years have seldom entered my mind.

Then, remembrance of Jesus' words: "Whosoever shall say, Thou fool, shall be in danger of hell fire" (Matt. 5:22). Not just "fool"—any derogatory name applied judgmentally and in anger to any soul for whom Christ died.

Then conviction: Oh, God, what's wrong with me? This has been happening to me more and more lately. I am becoming possessed by unrighteous anger. *Jesus, help. Jesus, take control. Don't let the evil one take over.*

And the still, small voice speaks: "You're in too much of a hurry. Keep within the speed limit. When it says seventy, it means seventy. Render unto Caesar. Intentionally going over seventy with no letups is different from occasionally and unintentionally slipping over the limit while watching the road. If you always consciously go beyond the limit—even if only a little—you will develop a frame of mind that affects your response to all laws, human and divine. You will eventually push against the edge of restraint in all things and rationalize a defense. The evil one will have you."

Silence.

Slowing to seventy.

Less tension. At peace with the state—and heaven. Not resentful of those who speed past me. No name-calling. Instead, a prayer for their safety. "Great peace have they which love thy law: and nothing shall offend them" (Ps. 119:165).

Staying under seventy and singing. *"Amazing grace! how sweet the sound ..." "Oh, to grace how great a debtor daily I'm constrained to be ..." "What wondrous love is this that caused the Lord of bliss to bear the dreadful curse for my soul ..." "I wonder as I wander, out under the sky, how Jesus the Savior did come for to die for poor ornery people like you and like I ..." "I'm just a poor wayfaring stranger, traveling through this world below, but way up yonder there's no sorrow in that fair land to which I go ..."*

Airport exit up ahead. Already?

Long-term parking. Northwest ticket counter. "My ticket is for the 12:50 flight to Detroit. Could I be on standby for the 11:15 flight?"

"How about taking the 10:00 a.m. flight? It has plenty of room and is boarding now at Gate B6. You have time to make it."

Thank You, Jesus.

So often, as we drive on blue highways through little towns, we find all the lights are green—if we go the right speed. In Christ it is "not yea and nay" (2 Cor. 1:19), but in Him, it is always yes. "For the Lord God is a sun and shield: the Lord will give grace and glory: no good thing will he withhold from them that walk uprightly" (Ps. 84:11).

I should not go beyond the speed limit anymore. Neither should I push beyond the edge of God's restraints.

So it seems to me.

# *What Katie Rivenbark Taught Us about Witnessing*

*There are two kinds of witnessing. Both are important.*

This is about Katie Rivenbark, four student colporteurs, and a decision not to witness to her.

Katie was a short, pleasant-faced widow who rented rooms in Wallace, North Carolina (population 843). We were selling Bibles and a book called *Drama of the Ages*, and we needed a place to stay for the summer. Overjoyed at having four roomers for three months, Katie was happy to turn most of her house over to us.

She watched us move in and put our girlfriends' pictures, our Bibles, and our Sabbath School quarterlies on the dressers. She watched as we headed out to get groceries and see about renting a post office box.

She joined us when we had worship. She said she was pleased to have Christian boys in her home. It was hard not to tell her who we were, to tell her what Jesus had done for us, but we were determined not to risk antagonizing our landlady. That summer, we were not going to witness to Katie Rivenbark.

Each day, we were long gone before she got up. We returned after dark, prepared supper, ate, cleaned the kitchen, had worship, and retired to our rooms to fill out daily reports and get ready for bed.

All went well until the weekend. Katie was puzzled when we came home at noon Friday, had lunch, gave the part of the house we used a thorough cleaning, and bought groceries for the week. She was puzzled when we gathered for sundown worship, puzzled when we left the next morning carrying Bibles and quarterlies instead of briefcases.

She was indignant when we didn't go to church on Sunday. "You're not very good Christians if you don't go to church," she said.

"We went to church yesterday," we had to explain. "We observe the Sabbath."

"Well, I'm a Presbyterian, and I've never heard of such a thing. I've read my Bible through sixteen times," she said. "You're supposed to keep the Lord's day."

For the rest of the summer, Katie was sharp with us.

She told us that if she had known we were Adventists, she would not have rented to us. But we stayed calm and friendly.

We did witness that summer to others. We had prayer in every home we visited, signed up people for the Bible correspondence course, and gave Bible studies to several families nearby, but we did not witness to Katie Rivenbark.

On the morning we left for college, we were packed and waiting for our ride. We thanked Katie for putting up with us, had prayer, and gave her a deluxe copy of *Drama of the Ages*. Inside the cover we had placed an application card for a Bible correspondence course.

Katie accepted our gift, but she said, "You can't stay at my place next summer." We said we were sorry she felt that way and told her goodbye. We had kept our pledge not to witness to our landlady.

Or had we?

College classes were in full swing when a letter came in early December from Wallace, N.C. "My life has been bettered by your spending the summer in Wallace," she wrote. "I want you boys to know I get a lot of understanding and pleasure out of the book you all gave me. I think it is about the best earthly gift I have ever had. I am still studying the Bible correspondence course. I hope you all did not think too hard of me for saying what I did about letting you stay here next summer. I am sorry I ever said it. You would be welcome. Your friend, Mrs. Katie Rivenbark."

And then in a letter about a year later: "Brother Bartocchini has been having Bible studies at my home each week. I will be baptized next Sabbath. Your friend in Christ, Mrs. Katie Rivenbark."

There are two kinds of witnessing. When you accept Jesus into your life, you can't help attracting others to Jesus. The other kind is consciously telling someone what Jesus has done for you, giving Bible studies, sharing literature. Both kinds are important. Four student colporteurs witnessed to Katie Rivenbark throughout the summer, even when we tried not to.

So it seems to me.

# *Company's Coming*

*Being Ready for Company.*
*Being Ready for*
*Jesus to Come.*

We had a parade of welcome visitors after we retired to Naples, Florida. Former students looked us up—one couple on their honeymoon. Former colleagues from Southern Adventist University, Andrews University, and Atlantic Union College. And long-lost relatives were found.

We enjoyed all our company. But sometimes it involved a lot of work if we knew ahead they were coming. Occasionally, guests dropped by unannounced or phoned from a rest stop on I-75 and gave us one or two hours' notice. That's when we wished we had been involved in a lot of work the previous day.

When we knew ahead, here's what we might have done:

Mow the lawn on Wednesday instead of putting it off until Friday.
Give the house a genteel cleaning. We vacuumed in the corners and under the furniture. Everything we could reach was dusted—even figurines and picture frames.

Make repairs. Once, I replaced our shabby doorbell with a shiny brass one with a small light that shines continually so that guests couldn't miss it. Too many people who had come to our door had not seen the doorbell and had knocked. If we were sitting in the lanai watching birds, we could not hear knuckle knocks as well as doorbell chimes.

Inspect the walls for smudges. If scrubbing didn't care for smudges, some leftover paint did.

Clear up clutter. If there wasn't time to put each item where it belongs, we would scoop it all up and put it in a box to go through later. Where to put the box? In a place called "garage." In south Florida where the water table is high, no one has basements. And because of the possibility of strong hurricane winds, seldom is a home built with an attic. What looks like a garage from the outside is really a basement disguised as a garage.

Weed the shrub beds.

Put in bedding plants. Once, when the heat of summer had ended six months of glorious impatiens blossoms, I pulled out all the wilting impatiens, rushed to Walmart, purchased two dozen caladiums, several bags of peat humus, and a bag of Osmocote, and filled in the empty section of the flower bed. I finished just in time to shower and put on clean clothes before our guests arrived. They were able to sit in the lanai, look out at our tropical backyard, and enjoy not only the shiny green of the citrus trees, the spears of the birds-of-paradise, and the gold of the crotons, but also the brilliant reds of the caladiums.

In summary, we did the equivalent of a northern spring cleaning—and more. That is, when we knew someone was coming.

But cleaning wasn't all.

We checked the cupboards. We bought more sweets than we usually stocked. If we knew our guests' special likes, we planned to serve their favorites. We also considered their dietary restrictions. We phoned a few restaurants to see what they were serving vegetarians. We could take our guests out a time or two.

We wanted them to come. We wanted them to have a great time in Naples and at our house. We wanted to have all our preparations finished before they arrived so we could enjoy their company.

We, therefore, encouraged them to let us know when they were coming. Preparing for them was like preparing for ourselves. We enjoyed the neat flower and shrub beds, the freshly mowed lawn, the house clear of clutter, the walls free of smudges, the bright caladiums. We liked to be ready before they arrived so we could sit in our lanai and enjoy our house and yard to the fullest before they came, while they were here, and even afterward.

We know Jesus is coming.

We should all put more effort into being ready for His coming than the coming of former students, colleagues, acquaintances, and long-lost relatives.

Being ready for Jesus also benefits us before His arrival. We enjoy life here so much more after we let Him prepare us for His coming.

So it seems to me.

> *Being ready for Jesus also benefits us before His arrival. We enjoy life here so much more after we let Him prepare us for His coming.*

# *Hurricane Preparation*

*We can be
prepared for the
storm that tries
our faith.*

How long does it take to prepare for a hurricane? Before we moved to Naples, Florida, we knew that tropical depressions came across the Atlantic from Africa, beginning in early June and lasting until late November. Any of those depressions could become a hurricane. The last one to hit Naples was Hurricane Donna in 1960.

Helen and I went through three hurricane seasons before we were completely prepared for a major hurricane to hit Naples. There were too many other things to do—get a Florida license plate (we chose the one with a manatee), arrange our furniture, unpack boxes, put up towel racks (we've never moved to a house that had enough towel racks.)

We did only three things to prepare for a hurricane that first season—obtain passes needed to reenter the county after an evacuation, pick up brochures, and attend a lecture.

When the next season rolled around, we had invested in roll-down shutters and steel panels to cover the windows.

During the following season, we developed a plan. During a category 1 or 2 hurricane, we would stay home. Our home could withstand 110-mile winds (we hoped), and the lot is higher than the expected tidal surge from the Gulf of Mexico. If a category 3 hurricane were likely, we would stay at Mother's. On higher ground, her condominium had withstood the winds and surge of Donna in 1960. If a category 4 or 5 hurricane were forecast, we would all go to an approved shelter or evacuate.

We packed enough nonperishable food and bottled water to last three days. We filled a container with a battery radio, flashlights, first-aid supplies, and a Bible. We kept a container on hand for important papers and a few family photos. We hired a company to see if our roof was sufficiently anchored and braced to withstand a category 4 or 5 hurricane (It wasn't).

We were waiting for bids from several carpenters when Hurricane Georges made headlines. With apprehension, we tracked it across Puerto Rico, the Dominican Republic, Haiti, and Cuba. It had caused much damage and loss of life and was headed directly for Naples. Since the wind had lost strength crossing the islands, we expected only a category 2 or 3 storm.

It was time to act. Get cash from the bank. Board up windows. Place boxes and small furniture on tables and beds. Too late to have the roof anchored and braced. Too late to purchase caps to cover the turbine vent holes on the roof. Too late to make a photo inventory of our belongings. But we were prepared enough to protect our lives, if not our possessions.

But Georges didn't visit Naples. After leaving Key West, it moved over the Gulf several hundred miles from our coast.

Next time it may be different. Before then, we'll be fully prepared. I already have vent caps. The work on the roof will soon be completed. And Helen is making a photo inventory of our belongings.

A different kind of storm is coming. Daniel refers to it as a "time of trouble, such as never was since there was a nation" (Dan. 12:1). Ellen White writes: "The storm is coming, relentless in its fury. Are we prepared to meet it?" (*Evangelism*, p. 199). We should be more serious about preparing for that storm than preparing for a hurricane. What is that preparation? It is planting our feet on the Rock of Ages and hiding ourselves in Jesus, our only refuge.

It took us three years to get ready for Georges, and we were not fully prepared then. How long will it take to prepare for the storm that will try our faith? If hiding ourselves in Jesus is top priority, it will take only long enough to accept His gift of grace—a wonderful exercise to be repeated continually. If it does not become top priority, we will never be prepared, no matter how many acts of piety and other partial preparations we make.

So it seems to me.

# N/A

*To the Christian,
the way of the
world is N/A.*

Frequently, I receive questionnaires. A marketing company wants to know how airlines can improve their frequent-flier programs. A professor is doing research for her next book. The Christian Coalition is taking a poll, hoping to influence Congress. I'm asked to respond with Strongly Agree, Agree, Disagree, Strongly Disagree; Yes, No, or Uncertain. Some of the answers can be N/A (Not Applicable). Often that's the only answer I can give.

When we moved to Florida, I learned that N/A is a response I also give to choices other than those on questionnaires.

Finding a good gardening book was hard when we lived in Tennessee. Most are written for people living near Lancaster, Pennsylvania. I amassed quite a collection of such books and tried to adapt the information to Tennessee. How exciting to find a title such as *Gardening in the South*. I learned that for peonies to bloom, the root crown should go through a freeze. Growing peonies in the Midsouth required that the crowns be planted nearly even with the surface--not two inches below, as all the regular garden books tell you. If the crown is planted two inches below the surface in Tennessee, it would likely miss getting frozen and fail to bloom.

Gardening in southern Florida is even more different. Instead of planting a vegetable garden in April and May, one plants in September and October. The summers are too hot and wet for most vegetables to do well in the summer. It is November as I write this, and our garden is doing well—tomatoes, peppers, eggplants, and others. I broke my resolve never to buy any more gardening books. I now have nineteen devoted to Florida gardening. The others were N/A.

Direct-mail advertising is seldom useful to me. It is less so in Florida. Catalogs feature winter clothes, warm coats, cashmere and cable-knit sweaters. N/A. Catalogs invite us to order oranges and grapefruit from California or Texas. N/A. We have our own citrus trees.

When Helen and I were students at Southern Adventist University (then Southern Missionary College), we had a teacher who frequently paraphrased Romans 12:2: "Be not conformed to the Tennessee way of life," Prof. Leif Tobiassen would say. "Don't let the Tennessee way of life squeeze you into its own mold." To the Christian, the way of the world is N/A.

We're frequently reminded of Prof. Tobiassen when telemarketers call, and catalogs arrive in the mail. Catalogs of pornographic videos are pitched into the trash. N/A.

"Mrs. Sauls, how are you today?" the telemarketer from Jacobson's Department Store gives herself away (no friend ever begins a phone conversation that way). "We're offering all newcomers to Naples a complete makeover—rouge, lipstick, eye shadow—free." N/A. We're not new to Naples anymore. And to Helen, the rouge, lipstick, and eye shadow are N/A.

"We'll give you a coffeemaker if you try our coffee for one month." N/A.

"We'll send you a free carton of cigarettes for filling out our questionnaire." N/A.

"Today, we're giving a free bottle of wine with every two entrée orders." N/A.

Some things are always applicable. "For God so loved the world, that he gave his only begotten Son, that whosoever believeth in him should not perish, but have everlasting life" (John 3:16). "Blessed are they which do hunger and thirst after righteousness: for they shall be filled" (Matt. 5:6).

"For the Lord God is a sun and shield: the Lord will give grace and glory: no good thing will he withhold from them that walk uprightly" (Ps. 84:11).

"Don't let the world around you squeeze you into its own mould," writes Paul, "but let God re-mould your minds from within, so that you may prove in practice that the plan of God for you is good" (Rom. 12:2, Phillips). We should cling to the applicables but not be conformed to many of the N/As.

So it seems to me.

# *Friends*

*What a hard
time members
would have
without friends.*

By the time Helen and I retired to Naples, Florida, we had been members of ten different Adventist churches through the years—from the small rural Floral Crest Seventh-day Adventist Church on Sand Mountain in northern Alabama to the large Collegedale, Tennessee, Church on the campus of Southern Adventist University, to the midsized Naples Church, whose attendance nearly doubles every winter. Four types of members make up each of the ten congregations, it seems to me.

- ★ The *unknowings* never call, never come to see us, seldom speak at church. They do not know us. And we have not had the opportunity to know them.
- ★ The *acquaintances* smile, shake hands, call us by name, and in some churches, give warm hugs. But they never call and never come to see us. Their friendliness at church is a nice ritual.

★ The *telemarketers* call frequently. They always want us to do something—bring a salad to the supper, tell the children's story next Sabbath, teach a Sabbath School lesson, order a cherry pie from Pathfinders, contribute to the building fund. These are all good things. And the telemarketers are effective in getting others involved. They themselves are very active in the church. I admire their dedication. But the only time they call is when they want something.

★ The *friends* smile, shake hands, call us by name, and give warm hugs at church. They call on us when they want something. But they also call or drop by to encourage, to affirm, and to invite us to do something with them.

"We missed you last Sabbath. Are you OK?"

"Lynn, I really liked your children's story about the peanut butter sandwich."

"Helen, when you were one of the elders on the platform last Sabbath, your pastoral prayer meant so much to me."

*Thank You, Lord, for the friends in the church.*

"Your 'Company's Coming' article in the *Review* helped me understand how being ready for Jesus makes life better now."

"Let's get together on New Year's Eve for a game of Scrabble."

"Come over and have supper with us Friday evening."

"Let's go walk the pier and watch the sun go down as the Sabbath ends. We'll drop by for you."

"I heard that you have been quite sick. Ted and I are praying for you."

Thank You, Lord, for the friends in the church. I love the message. I love Jesus and the blessed hope. But if the church were made up of just the unknowings, the acquaintances, and the telemarketers, something special about being a member of the church would be missing.

And what a hard time new members would have without friends in the church. Some of them are having problems at work because they are now keeping the Sabbath. Some are facing pressure from relatives who feel they have been brainwashed by a cult. Some are lonely because their new lifestyle has alienated many of their old friends. The unknowings, the acquaintances, and the telemarketers aren't helping them cope. But the friends in the church are.

We don't all have the same spiritual gifts. But we can look for the spiritual gifts in others and let them know how we appreciate what they are doing. Paul counsels all of us to "be kindly affectioned one to another." To be "given to hospitality." To "rejoice with them that do rejoice, and weep with them that weep" (Rom. 12:10,13,15).

More encouragement, expressions of appreciation, and gifts of time and fellowship instead of apathy, criticism, and accusation would do a lot to bring unity to our churches. If the unknowings, acquaintances, and telemarketers could become friends, others would be led to a closer walk with Jesus and be bonded to the church.

Come to think of it, I should be a friend to some of the unknowings, to some of the acquaintances, and to some of the telemarketers. I should phone one of them tonight.

So it seems to me.

# Jesus and Journalists

*Every Christian is
a Journalist.*

Shortly after I began teaching journalism at Andrews University, my wife, Helen, handed me an article from a *Good Housekeeping* magazine. "Look at this," she said. It was an article based on the answers Lawrence Eisenberg received when he asked well-known TV journalists whom they would most like to interview—living or dead—and what they would like to ask.[2]

Eisenberg asked the question to such journalists as Walter Cronkite, Barbara Walters, Dan Rather, Maria Shriver, and Tom Brokaw. They gave such answers as Gandhi, Moses, Robert E. Lee ("His decision to leave the union, and looking back, whether he thought the great destruction of the Civil War was, in fact, worth it," said Roger Mudd), Jacqueline Kennedy Onassis ("Because she gives no interviews," said Barbara Walters), Mother Teresa, Thomas Jefferson, Napoleon, Pope John Paul II.

The name given most frequently was Jesus. Joan Lunden said, "I'd like to ask Jesus Christ, 'How are we all doing?'"

---

[2] "Who Would You Most Like to Interview—And What Would You Ask?" *Good Housekeeping*, October 1986, pp. 56–58.

Maria Shriver said, "I'd like to ask Jesus Christ how He managed to keep His faith in the face of such adversity."

Tom Brokaw's answer was short: "Jesus Christ—for all the obvious reasons."

Journalists, for the most part, are a skeptical bunch. They are skeptical of the supernatural and of organized religion. And yet, 2,000 years after Jesus appeared in history, He is the one they most wanted to interview.

There's a reason, it seems to me, that He is the most newsworthy person to step across the pages of history. Not *Time's* Man of the Year. Not the most influential person of the century or the millennium. But *Time's* Man of All Time.

The message of Jesus Christ is called the gospel or the good news. But the word "news" occurs only once in the Bible: "As cold waters to a thirsty soul, so is good news from a far country" (Prov. 25:25). The text is a summary of the whole Bible. It is a summary of Jesus' mission. Heaven is the far country. Jesus is the good news from that far country. His Word is the Newspaper, the Newscast, the Newsmagazine.

It is in the very nature of humans to thirst for news. When we see someone we haven't seen for a while, we ask, "What's new?" We watch CNN News again and again and ask ourselves, "Why am I still watching this? It's almost a complete repetition of the last half hour." The satisfaction of receiving earthly news is short-lived. God made us this way for a reason. Our thirst for news will draw us to Him. Our deepest need can be satisfied only as we accept the news from the Far Country and allow Jesus to quench our soul's thirst.

The most newsworthy event in all history, it seems to me, is the resurrection of Jesus. The most dramatic moment of that event was captured by journalist John Mark, who interviewed the women who had come to the empty tomb. The angel they met at the tomb had said to them, "He is risen; He is not here" (Mark 16:6). I don't believe Jesus would be the person most journalists would want to interview if He had not risen. He would have been merely one among thousands of religious teachers. His followers would not have turned the world upside down during the first century without the certainty of the resurrection. Nor would His followers today continue to carry with power the everlasting gospel to every nation, kindred, tongue, and people without that certainty.

Every Christian is a journalist with a special privilege, it seems to me. Jesus has granted each of us an interview. He wants us to interview Him every day. We can interview Him when we have devotions. The answers to our most important questions are in His Word. We can interview Him at any moment of the day. If we listen, He will speak to us through His still, small voice. As journalists, we can then report to others the good news from a Far Country.

So it seems to me.

# *Grapefruit, Ice, and Oxygen*

*The natural world*

*is a mystery.*

God is a mystery. We cannot see Him. We cannot directly experience Him through our senses. The natural world, which we can see, hear, smell, taste, and feel, is also a mystery.

Helen and I discovered the mystery of grapefruit when we moved to Naples. From our Florida room, we can see two large grapefruit trees. The limbs of one droop toward the ground each fall weighed down with pink fruit; the limbs of the other droop with golden fruit. If the fruit is picked, it won't keep as well as when left on the tree. At room temperature it will keep only for a week or so before it begins to shrivel and decompose. If it is stored in the refrigerator crisper, it will keep for a month before losing its flavor. If it is left on the tree, however, it will keep fresh and sweet for a number of months, the pink from November through May, the one with the lighter flesh through June—even in 90-degree heat. A biologist could explain *how* this works, but *why* it works this way is a mystery. And a welcome one.

Ice, it seems to me, is one of the best examples of the mysteries of the natural world. Nearly everything in its solid state is heavier than in its liquid state. Water is an exception: ice floats. And it's a good thing; otherwise, it would form on the bottoms of most lakes, ponds, and larger bodies of water in one winter and destroy the plant and animal life there. The warmth of spring and summer would be insufficient to melt that ice, insulated as it would be from the sun's rays.

In a few years, the lakes and rivers of much of the world would be frozen solid. A few more years and the globe would be a mass of ice. Nearly everything in its solid state is heavier than in its liquid state. But ice floats. Is not a powerful, intelligent, loving God the answer to this mystery?

But how to accept the mystery of a God we cannot see?

Consider oxygen, one of the most abundant elements on earth. It is the substance most vital to life on this planet. In spite of its abundance and importance, it was unknown until 200 years ago, when Joseph Priestley, an English scientist, demonstrated its existence.

Until then, we humans had been unaware of the substance most vital to our very existence. If separated from it, we can lose consciousness in five minutes, experience brain damage in eight minutes, and die in fifteen minutes. Yet humans did not know about it until 200 years ago.

This is not too surprising when we realize that oxygen cannot be directly perceived through the senses. We cannot see it or smell it or taste it. Only when it is isolated can we weigh it. We know of its existence mainly through what it does when combined with other elements. When it combines with iron, it forms rust. When it combines with combustible material, it makes fire. When it combines with red blood cells in the human body, it keeps us alive.

We are also surrounded this moment by God's presence and have been all our lives. He is around us, seeking entrance into our hearts. If we allow Him, He becomes part of us. If we are separated from Him by doubt, neglect, or waywardness, our lives can become chaotic, we can lose hope, and life can become meaningless.

Though God is everywhere, often, we do not discern Him. We cannot see Him any more than we can see oxygen. We cannot directly experience His presence through our senses. But He brings us again and again to discover Him. We can see Him in His works. We see His concern for us in the floating ice on a New England pond. In silence we can hear Him knock upon the doors of our hearts. We hear Him call as we discern the needs of others and realize that as we serve them, we serve Him. The Word became flesh and dwelt among us. His Word helps us know and demonstrate that in His presence is fullness of joy, and at His right hand are pleasures for evermore (see Ps. 16:11).

So it seems to me.

# *Through a Glass Darkly*

*All of us see through a glass darkly—*
*some more than others.*

When she died, I recalled four good things about Maria:[3]

1. *She loved children.* She would get down on the floor with her young son and her nephews and nieces and teach them to draw. Then, since there was no money to buy crayons, she would take them for a walk in the meadow to pick flowers. She taught them how to mash and rub the petals on the paper to color the pictures they had drawn.
2. *She was a nurturing mother.* She read to her children, and from their youngest days, encouraged them to get a college education even though she had dropped out of high school.
3. *She was generous.* She often sent gifts to her parents and five sisters, and her husband's parents. She showered her son and

---
[3] A pseudonym.

daughter-in-law with gifts—Hummels and other collectibles, an antique German clock, paintings.
4. *She liked to grow things.* Until her health broke, her yard was filled with flowers, and her vegetable garden supplied neighbors with produce.

In spite of these good things, I had sometimes wondered whether or not she was demon-possessed. Here's why:

1. *She took things that did not belong to her—even when she did not need them.* From stores. From neighbors. Even from relatives.
2. She *was unpredictable.* She would take offense when no offense was intended and respond with abusive language. In a restaurant she often felt that people were staring at her and would yell out: "Stare like a maniac!"
3. *She was dishonest.* She'd say preposterous things to make her relatives think that she was sick, abused, or destitute when all was well—other than her warped state of mind.
4. *She was often violent.* Her first husband carried scars from when she went after him with a butcher knife. Once, when she was upset with her husband, she threw her two-year-old son on the floor. When she got upset over something, she would throw dishes and figurines.
5. *She was manipulative.* If she could not get others to do what she wanted by being sweet and winsome, she would try lying, abusive language, violence, and suicide threats. Her children and her husband would do almost anything to prevent her temper tantrums.

Her first husband had to leave after fifteen years of marriage. Her two sons left home when they were still in high school. Her second husband did not put up with her tantrums. Now and then, he had her spend time in a psychiatric ward. Except for brief periods away from home, he stayed with her nearly fifty years. She was in a nursing home the last four months of her life. He visited her every day. His patience could render him a candidate for sainthood.

At the time of her death, two texts came to mind that gives me hope of seeing Maria again: "For now we see through a glass, darkly; but then face to face: now I know in part; but then shall I know even as also I am known" (1 Cor. 13:12).

All of us see through a glass darkly—some more darkly than others. Maria's negative behavior, it seems to me, resulted from her not seeing things clearly, from greatly mixed-up DNA.

The thief on the cross who asked Jesus to remember him when Jesus came into His kingdom evidently had mixed up DNA. Because the thief turned to Jesus, does not 1 Corinthians 15:52 apply to him? "In a moment, in the twinkling of an eye, at the last trumpet … [he] shall be changed" —his DNA will be restored to perfection.

Nearly everyone has a friend or loved-one like Maria. Jesus counsels against judging them. We are not capable of judging because we all see through a glass darkly. And they may behave the way they do because their vision is clouded—their DNA was mixed up.

*All of us see through a glass darkly— some more darkly than others.*

We can take hope because God is merciful. He considers where we were born (see Ps. 87:4, 6). He considers how our perception of reality is flawed because of heredity and environment. He knows whether or not we would have spurned His grace if we could have seen more clearly.

How can such sinners as we fit into heaven and the new earth? All our DNA is mixed up. Jesus helps some of it get straightened out now, and at his second coming will restore us completely "in a moment, in the twinkling of an eye."

Only God knows whether or not I'll get to see Maria again. But I hope that I shall—if then neither she nor I will see through a glass darkly, but will know even as we are known.

So it seems to me.

# *Angels*

*Their angelic
ministry made
a difference in
my life.*

Some people have seen angels. I haven't. But some of the human guardians and messengers God has sent my way—and their angelic ministry—have made a difference in my life.

Papa (that's what I called my grandfather Sauls) prayed before meals, read his Bible, and was a pillar in the rural Missionary Baptist Church. He loved children and was forever finding ways to demonstrate that he loved me.

Maniece (that's what I called my maternal grandmother), a good Christian Scientist, taught me that "God is love," that a positive attitude is better than a negative one, and that as a person "thinketh in his heart, so is he" (Prov. 23:7).

The happiest period of my rather unsettled childhood was the summer between first and second grade. We lived two miles from the Hollywood,

Florida, beach. Overcome by depression that summer, my mother stayed in bed. But she let me go to the beach every day. Sometimes I walked; sometimes I hitchhiked. Sometimes I took a sack lunch, sometimes I gathered pop bottles and used the return deposits to buy junk food.

Then I met Rex. He did not smoke or drink. He could turn a complete flip and land on his feet. He and his buddies had come to Hollywood waiting to be drafted into the armed services prior to World War II. That summer, Rex taught me to swim and to eat right (milk instead of soda pop, fruit instead of candy) and used his influence to get me on the Hollywood swimming team as their mascot. When he went into the Air Force, he left a healthier, happier little boy in Hollywood.

A couple of years later, we moved to a different neighborhood. Mr. Barwick lived two houses away. Early Sunday morning, he would drive around, see children playing, and ask if they wanted to go to Sunday School and church. Those of us who were interested crowded into the Barwicks' family car and went to the First Baptist Church. We especially liked to go to BTU (Baptist Training Union) Sunday evening because on the way home, Mr. Barwick treated us to ice-cream sundaes. As best I knew how I wanted to be on God's side and have so chosen ever since.

Once, when my mother was in the hospital for an extended stay, my father let me take a bus from Hollywood to Homestead all by myself to see Aunt Mitt, Uncle Byrd, and Cousin Jenny. Aunt Mitt was one of my angels. She was so exuberant in her affirmation that I could read it in her voice, her smile, and the twinkle of her eyes. It was a memorable weekend. I first became aware of Seventh-day Adventists on that trip. As we drove by a little stone church, people were coming out of the building. It was Saturday. "Look at those Seventh-day Adventists," said Uncle Byrd. "They keep Saturday for Sunday."

Back at the Sauls' home place in Georgia, I attended Sunday School every week at the Freewill Baptist Church just down the road. Mrs. Pete Aycock was the young people's teacher. And she was a good one. She motivated us to memorize the Beatitudes, Psalm 1, Psalm 23, 1 Corinthians 13, and the Ten Commandments. She gave us presents at Christmas. After I moved away, she corresponded with me until she couldn't write anymore and had to go to a nursing home.

Two school teachers were angels to me. Family life was so dysfunctional during my first two years of school that I had a hard time learning. Miss Slater, my third- and fourth-grade teacher, turned this poor reader into a good one, gave me a love for learning, and helped me have a mind open to new ideas. Miss Johnson, my high school trigonometry and solid geometry teacher, was as interested in her students' welfare as their mastery of math. She listened attentively as I told her about my family problems.

How helpful Pastor Glenn Henrickson and his wife were to me while I was deciding to become a Seventh-day Adventist. They opened their home to me every weekend and took me 500 miles to see Southern Missionary College (now Southern Adventist University). During my six years at that college, I found wonderful guardians in many of my teachers and classmates. I became better acquainted with Jesus.

As God sends angels to guard and instruct, so He sends humans. He wants us to be guardians and messengers to the children and youth around us. We can make an eternal difference in their lives.

So it seems to me.

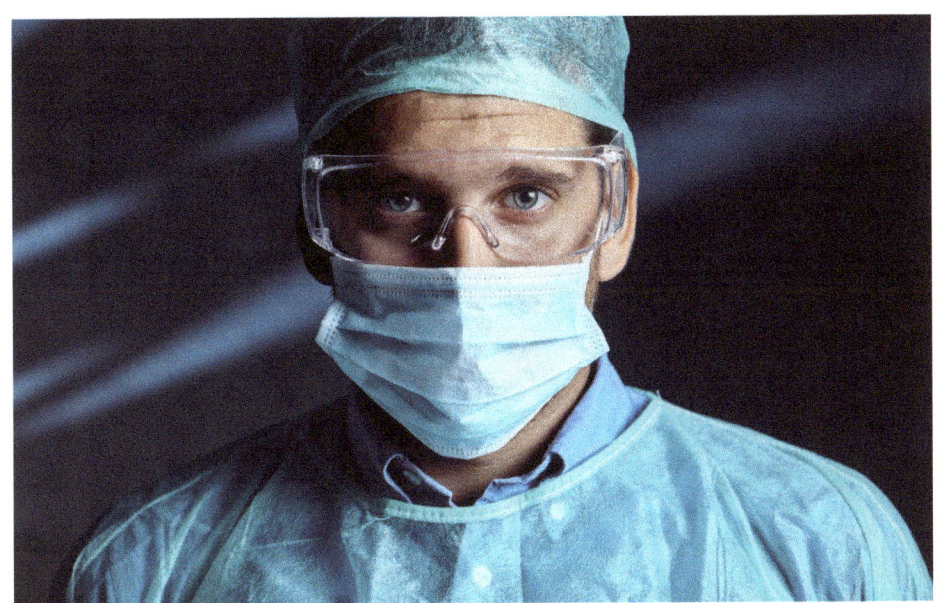

# *You Never Know — That Child Might Grow Up to Be a Heart Surgeon*

*Sow kindness;*
*reap kindness.*

The summer heat distracted Helen and me from our studies that first Sunday in Iowa City. We were on a leave of absence from Southern Missionary College (now Southern Adventist University) for graduate work at the University of Iowa. Our class assignments were interesting, but we were tired from the move—especially the heat.

The heat, however, was not the only distraction. The woman in the next house—only ten feet away—had all her windows open. She sat by her window typing to the rhythm of a Baroque symphony, the volume of the hi-fi so loud our windows rattled.

"I can't concentrate," said Helen.

My options:

1. Get out the Tennessee Ernie Ford record that Helen's father gave us and turn the volume up as high as it would go. Then, out of self-defense, our neighbor might stop invading our space with her stereo.
2. Have our seven-year-old son take over a note asking her to lower the volume.

Bad options. The first would alienate. The second would be cowardly.

So I picked out a favorite Vivaldi LP and, with trepidation, visited our neighbor. A small woman with smiling eyes answered the door.

"We love Baroque music," I said. "But the sound amplifies so much between our houses we can't concentrate on our studies. I wonder if you could turn the volume down a bit. Oh, and have you heard this one?" I held out the LP.

"I would love to hear it," she said. "And I have some I think you would like. Oh, my, I do have it a bit loud. I'll turn it down right now." After she returned with two records, I learned she would be one of my professors. I shudder to think what might have happened.

We should always be kind—out of self-interest if for no other reason. That kid next door who out-menaces Dennis the Menace might be your boss someday. That nerdy classmate might someday be one of your child's teachers. That bratty cousin might be closer to you in a few years than any of your other eighty-seven cousins. Beware of road rage. That driver who upset you might be the oncologist you go to when an MRI shows you have a suspicious-looking growth in your abdomen. Sow kindness; reap kindness. If we hope to win others to Jesus, we must treat them kindly.

Last Sabbath, someone new came to Sabbath School. Where had I seen him before? "This is my first time here," he said. When he gave his name and told me he was in real estate, I remembered where we had met. In one of our apartments. He had considered renting and then subletting it to a client from Germany. Although I had concerns about subletting, I had treated him kindly. "I didn't know you were a Sabbath-keeper," he said as he joined me. He belonged to the Seventh-day Church of God and had come to worship with us since he had no church home in Naples. How glad I am that I had been kind to him.

The watchword for evangelism is Kindness. "If we would … be kind and courteous …," writes Ellen White, "there would be one hundred conversions to the truth where now there is only one" (*Testimonies for the Church,* vol. 9, p. 189).

Christians who have been born again and are growing in grace will become kind—not from ulterior motives but because kindness will eventually be to them as natural as breathing. When Jesus said, "Be ye therefore perfect, even as your Father which is in heaven is perfect" (Matt. 5:48), He was referring to God's type of kindness. The preceding passage presents a heavenly Father who makes His "sun to rise on the evil and on the good, and sendeth rain on the just and on the unjust" (verse 45). In the parallel sermon recorded in Luke, Jesus said, "But love ye your enemies, and do good, ... and ye shall be the children of the Highest: for he is kind unto the unthankful and to the evil. Be ye therefore merciful, as your Father also is merciful" (Luke 6:35–36).

I long for the day when it will be natural to be kind. Until then, I will try to be kind even when annoyed. You never know—that adolescent next door might show up in church some Sabbath or grow up to be a heart surgeon and save my life.

So it seems to me.

# *Longevity*

*As a fine
violin ages, its
tones become
more brilliant.*

Things that last a long time intrigue us. More so today than even in the 1960s when the restaurants T.G.I. Fridays and Cracker Barrel with their nineteenth-century decor began. Antiques Roadshow remains one of the most popular public television programs. Viewers enjoy seeing how a small table found at a yard sale for $25 is valued at $30,000 because of its age. When my wife, Helen, and I discovered Naples, Florida, in 1977, it had three antique shops. Now it has seventy.

Violins, violas, and cellos age well. Antonio Stradivari made more than 1,000 between 1658 and 1737. Nearly 600 still exist. As a fine violin ages, its tones become fuller and more brilliant.[4]

---

[4] Some facts for this article were taken from Frank Kendig and Richard Hutton's *Life Spans: Or How Long Things Last* (New York: Holt, Rinehart and Winston, 1980).

Trees are among the oldest living things. Bald cypresses live more than 600 years. The Corkscrew Swamp Sanctuary near Naples has some that were centenarians when Columbus discovered America. Redwoods live 1,000 years, giant sequoias 2,500 years, and bristlecone pines 3,000 years. No wonder the Bible uses a tree to represent longevity. "For as the days of a tree, so shall be the days of My people, and My elect shall long enjoy the work of their hands" (Isa. 65:22, NKJV).

Some small plants seem to last forever because they multiply by dividing. In a field in Lancaster, Massachusetts, is the site of the garrison house where Mary Rowlandson lived in 1675 when it was burned during King Phillip's war, and she was taken captive. Horseradishes from her garden still grew at the site when Helen and I taught at Atlantic Union College. Tawny daylilies colonists brought from Europe still thrive along roadsides throughout the eastern United States.

*As a fine violin ages, its tones become more brilliant.*

We like to visit old homes. A favorite of American visitors to England is the cottage in Chalfont St. Giles, where John Milton lived when he completed *Paradise Lost* in 1667. Helen and I were amazed when we had teacakes at Sally Lunn's in Bath, England, to learn that food has been served there since 1482.

The ancients made things to last. The Egyptians erected the pyramids and Great Sphinx in Egypt, and the Greeks erected the Parthenon in Athens long before Jesus was born. The Romans built the Colosseum during the first century as well as aqueducts, which still carry water.

Europeans in the Middle Ages also erected buildings to last. Chartres Cathedral was completed between 1194 and 1260. After 700 years, the blue of the stained glass is still brilliant.

New England farmers who erected stone walls over a period of 250 years built lasting monuments without intending to. They didn't know what else to do with the stones cleared from the land. More stones and sweat went into those walls than into the pyramids.

We are impressed by long-lasting marriages and consider a fiftieth anniversary something special. We are also impressed when someone reaches a one-hundredth birthday. Americans want to make life last longer. A lot of research goes into longevity. But any life span hoped for is short in comparison to those of the antediluvian patriarchs. Most of them lived 800 or 900 years; Methuselah lived the longest—969 years (see Gen. 5).

Imagine an endless straight line running through Naples. Southward it goes over Key West, Cuba, Panama, and out beyond the farthest reaches of the universe. Northward it goes over Jacksonville; Bristol, Tennessee; Cleveland, Ohio; and out beyond the farthest reaches of the universe. That line represents eternity.

Now place a small dot on that line. It represents the history of Earth. Our life spans are an infinitesimal part of that dot. They are but a puff, unless ... "Yes, God loved the world so much that he gave his only Son, so that everyone who believes in him may not be lost but may have eternal life" (John 3:16, Jerusalem). "God has given us eternal life and this life is in his Son" (1 John 5:11, Jerusalem).

Accepting God's gift is the best way to increase longevity.

So it seems to me.

# *Throw It into the Garbage Can*

*We listen to the
voice of middle-
class culture.*

When Helen and I taught at Southern Missionary College (now Southern Adventist University), we frequently visited the Great Smoky Mountains National Park to watch black bears. In those days, bears came out of the mountains to raid garbage cans in the camping and picnic areas. Bearproof garbage cans had not yet been invented.

The first time my parents visited us, we took them to the Smokies. Late afternoon we drove the winding road up the mountain between Gatlinburg and Newfound Gap looking for bear. We slowed down at each picnic area to see if a bear had come out of the woods to raid a garbage can. We drove all the way to Newfound Gap without seeing one. Then we turned around and started back down. A cluster of people looking down a bank let us know that a bear had been sighted. Too late. We got only a glimpse of a huge black bear. It had finished raiding that garbage can and was on its way to the next one.

We sped down the mountain, wanting to get to the next picnic area before the bear. "Get out some Little Debbie cakes," I said. "We'll get to the next garbage can before the bear does, put the cakes in the can, sit safely in our car, and watch it." I drove faster.

"But the signs say 'Don't Feed the Bears,'" said Helen.

"Oh, we won't do that. We could get an arm torn off. Bears can become dangerous if people hand food to them. But there's no law against feeding garbage cans."

Around the next hairpin curve was the picnic area. Three couples were standing around the tailgate of a station wagon parked a little distance from the far end of the picnic area. A garbage can was set just over the edge of the lot about fifteen feet from where the station wagon was parked. The couples had spread out their supper on the tailgate—a large container of Southern fried chicken, nearly a dozen sandwiches, and a big container of punch. No other vehicle was in the area.

We pulled in directly in front of the garbage can. As I opened the car door and ran out with the Little Debbie cakes, my mother spotted the bear coming out of the woods at the far end of the lot. With fear and excitement in her voice, she yelled to me, "A bear is coming! Hurry! Put the food in the garbage can."

The people looked up and saw the bear. They thought my mother had been talking to them and did exactly what she said. They threw all of their supper into the garbage can—the container of chicken, the sandwiches, even the punch. Then they dashed into their station wagon, closed the doors, rolled up the windows, and drove off just as the bear got to the garbage can to dine on what was probably the best meal it had ever discovered.

We watched for twenty minutes as the big bear poked its head down into the can time after time to pull up sandwiches, pieces of fried chicken, and finally, the Little Debbie cakes we had placed there for it.

Watching the bear was fun. And though we felt bad that we had been the partial cause of six people losing their supper, we couldn't help laughing at how they had obeyed, without thinking, a message from someone they did not know to throw away what was of value to them.

As I have considered the incident through the years, a parallel application has made me more serious. God has prepared a banquet for us. We are to feast on His Word. We are to feast on the bread broken for us, and the new wine poured out for us. He has given us the best that heaven has to offer. "This is My beloved Son," says the Father. "Hear Him!" (Matt. 17:5, NKJV).

We often listen to other voices. The voice of middle-class culture: "Put all your effort into living a life that is easy, pleasant, and respectable." The voice of a speed-addicted culture: "Hurry! Make life more action-packed with fast computers, fast food, fast news, instant best-sellers, quick-cut CDs, fast lanes. Make being busy your status symbol." All too often, we obey those voices, and neglect time with God, time alone, time with our families, time for devotions, time to delight in the Sabbath. Throwing away the banquet Jesus has prepared for us is a greater mistake than three couples obeying a message not intended for them and throwing their supper into a garbage can.

So it seems to me.

## *Christmas Is for All*

*Christmas
reminds us
that God cares
for us.*

Babies born since last Christmas have come into a world where evil dwells. But they don't know it yet. Like innocent babes of Bethlehem, they do not know they have been born to die. Neither do they know why green trees have been brought inside during the past few weeks, why lights have been strung, why the smells of cookies permeate the house, why presents have been wrapped in bright paper and placed under the tree.

Christmas is for them. It is because a special Baby was born 2,000 years ago that these little ones live in a world of hope, not just a world of sin, disappointment, and death. As the babes of Bethlehem were slain by Herod in place of the infant Jesus, so Jesus later was slain for them. He was slain for the little ones who are experiencing their first Christmas.

Christmas is for older children and young people who will experience their third, fourth, fifth, or even sixteenth Christmas this year. Their lives have been measured in Sabbaths and in Christmases. From Sabbath to Sabbath, they have been developing. From Christmas to Christmas, they are growing up.

Christmas is for workers, for them to get away from work for a few days. Come unto Him all you who labor and are heavy laden, and He will give you rest. Like those shepherds who left their flocks, they can leave their jobs for a few days and come even unto Bethlehem and remember Him who gave dignity to labor by growing up as a carpenter.

Christmas is for students. Like the Magi who left their stargazing and their scrolls, they can leave their tests and books and classes and follow the star to Bethlehem. There they can bow down and worship the Source of all wisdom.

Christmas is for parents, a time for them to do things for their children. A time to take time with them. To go shopping with them. To decorate the Christmas tree with them. To wrap gifts with them—and for them. To bake cookies and cakes and pies for them. To gather them around and read to them, tell them of past Christmases, and tell them the story of Jesus.

Then, when Christmas Day is over, and the children are in bed, it is time for parents to linger by the Christmas tree in silence and thank God for their children. And thank God for sending Jesus. Like quiet Joseph and gentle Mary, they can ponder all these things in their hearts.

> *Christmas is for those who are longing for Jesus to come again.*

Christmas is also for us older people—more so than for anyone else, it seems to me. At this time of year, we are forced to realize that Christmas comes around more frequently than it used to; that each Christmas brings us nearer to the time we will have to let go of the gifts we have received—the taste of cool water, the smell of spruce or pine, the sound of birds singing, the feel of beach sand on the feet, the pleasure of crawling between clean sheets to rest after a busy day. As Christmases come and go, we recognize that we must soon leave all these things.

But Christmas tells us more—if we believe in Jesus. We can have eternal life because of that first Christmas. We will not have to leave forever the things God gave us dominion over. Because of Christmas, there will be new heavens and a new earth.

Like Simeon and Anna, we older people are the ones who really can understand and appreciate Christmas. We are the ones who can say with

Simeon, "Lord, now you are letting Your servant depart in peace … for my eyes have seen Your salvation" (Luke 2:29–30 NKJV).

Some of our friends and loved ones who were alive last Christmas are no longer with us. It is especially hard to face this fact. Christmas has for us a touch of deep sadness. But it can also be a time of hope. Christmas reminds us that Jesus cares for us; that He has borne our griefs and carried our sorrows, that He suffered and died for us, that He is the resurrection and the life.

Christmas is for those who are longing for Jesus to come again.

So it seems to me.

# *Country Roads*

*Take Me Home*
*To the Place*
*Where I Belong*[5]

Sabbath School over. I find a place with the others in a pew facing the covered table. As I wait for the elders, deacons, and deaconesses to enter, I remember participating in my first ordinance of humility after I became an Adventist. I forgot the name of the man who washed my feet, but I'll never forget what he said. As he dried my feet, he looked down at them, smiled, and said, "Someday, these feet will walk the streets of gold." Suddenly, reality broke through to this former Christian Scientist: Heaven was a real place. It was more than just the title of a Bible study.

I also remembered the Communion Sabbath when out-of-town visitors sat in front of us. "No thanks," the woman said to the deacon as he reached out to serve her and her husband. "We had Communion at our

---

[5] "Take Me Home, Country Roads," by Bill Danoff, Taffy Nivert, and John Denver. Copyright 1971 Cherry Lane Music Co. Used by permission. All rights reserved.

church last Sabbath." She must have thought that celebrating the Lord's Supper more than once a quarter was a violation of church doctrine.

"That's all right," the deacon responded with a smile. "'For as often as ye eat this bread, and drink this cup, ye do show the Lord's death till he come.'"[6]

I also remember the Friday night party in celebration of Jesus one spring. It was held in the Gate quarters of the Boston Temple, where Adventist students operated a drop-in center on Saturday nights. As we entered the narrow door, someone rubber-stamped a have-a-happy face on our wrists. After putting together a montage about death and life and then assembling box posters, we sat at the cablespool tables, on the floor, or wherever and read scriptures, prayed, and sang. I remember that Carla read James Weldon Johnson's "Go Down, Death."

Toward the end of the evening, the pastor talked about Jesus breaking bread with the disciples who walked the country road to Emmaus. Then the pastor took a large loaf and broke it in half. From one half, he tore a small piece, placed it in the mouth of one sitting near him, and gave him the half loaf, starting it around the circle. Moving to another group, he started the other half.

As we served one another, passing the bread along, we sang, "Let Us Break Bread Together." Billy, a student from Jamaica, caught my eyes. Alan, a longish-haired junior from Canada, was also there. Red-haired Linda from Maine, wearing her granny dress, played her guitar and taught us the Appalachian spiritual, "Come, Ye Sinners." Doctors from New England Memorial Hospital were there. Nurses. Preachers. Teachers. Students. Old. Young. Black. Asian. White. It was altogether. Jesus was there.

That's what the Lord's Supper is all about. It's a road to take us home to the place where we belong. It takes us to that night long ago where Jesus girded Himself with humanity, washed our tired and dusty feet, and invited us to join Him in His cosmic act of ministry. That's where we belong.

It also leads us to that great banquet when we'll all be together at His table, and He'll drink grape juice with us. We'll sing, "Worthy is the Lamb, the Lamb that was slain, to receive all power and wealth, wisdom and might, honour and glory and praise!" (Rev. 5:12, NEB).

And that's also where we belong.

So it seems to me.

---

[6] 1 Corinthians 11:26.

# *Christian Meditation 101*

*"Let the words of my mouth,
and the meditation of my heart,
Be acceptable in thy sight,
O L*ORD*, my strength, and
my Redeemer" (Ps. 19:14).*

Christian meditation is taking time to realize that I am in God's presence and that in His presence are pleasures forevermore. That whether I am washing pots and pans, mowing a lawn, writing a letter, or talking with a friend, I am in God's presence. That by doing whatever I need to do, if I do it with zest and love, I am glorifying Him and worshipping Him. That when I consciously enjoy a slice of watermelon, a mango, or a slice of Boston cream pie, I am praising God and giving thanks to Him.

    Christian meditation is looking at the world around me and taking time to realize that even though it is a world in rebellion, it is still God's world. That even with its sin, violence, and misery, it, nevertheless, has so much order, so much beauty, so much goodness that I am happy to be in it, I am happy to be alive.

Christian meditation is looking at all the people around me and taking time to realize that they are God's children. That He made them in His image. That though they are fallen, though their physical and spiritual perfection is marred, Jesus loves them, has died for them, and wants to restore His image in every one of them. That all the true happiness they experience, the wisdom they possess, the goodness and kindness they manifest come from Him who lights every person who comes into the world.

Christian meditation is taking time to realize that I, too, belong to Jesus. That I am destined by His grace to enjoy Him forever. That He has given me the freedom to become like Him. That He knows my name, for it is graven on the palms of His hands. That I am important. That what I do matters. That if I choose not to be saved, there will be forever a lonely spot in the heart of Jesus.

Christian meditation is taking time to know that God is love. That He is bringing all things around to harmony. That right will win out. That even if the world's economy collapses, even if a persecuting political coalition takes over, even if a terrorist nuclear power breaks the globe in two, God is still working things out. He will bring it to pass that sin, misery, and hate will end, and love and goodness will reign forever.

Christian meditation is spending a thoughtful period of time each day thinking about some point in the life of Jesus. Taking time to concentrate on how He came and walked these roads, stubbed His toes, became thirsty the same as we do, enjoyed a drink of cold water the same as we do, knew what it was like to be tired, knew what it was like to be lonely, what it was like to be misunderstood, what it was like to weep, to be afraid, to be rejected, knew what it was like to be crucified, what it was like to rise after three days, victorious over Satan. He rejoices over every sinner who accepts His grace. He will come again with His angels to take His children to their heavenly home.

Christian meditation is taking time to be silent. Taking time to be still and to know that God is. It is being sorry for doing wrong. It is looking unto Jesus for forgiveness and faith. It is receiving grace and power from Him to overcome temptation. It is taking time to let the law of the Lord convert the soul, taking time to let the testimony of the Lord make wise the simple, taking time to let the statutes of the Lord rejoice the heart, taking time to let the commandments of the Lord enlighten the eyes (see Ps. 19:7–8).

Christian meditation is something to do under blue skies, under gray skies, under green trees. Something to do alone some starlit night. Something to do while waiting for a friend. Something to do while lying awake at night. Something to do in the morning, looking up at the ceiling with eyes wide open before getting up from the warm bed.

And now as we begin a new day, a new week, or a New Year, let the meditations of our hearts be acceptable in Your sight, O Lord, our strength and our Redeemer.

# *Meditation on Green*

*Green is the
Color of Go.*

Green is the color of morning meditation. When you wake up in summer before dawn and walk around a park or a city block or the campus, a few streetlights and the stars and the moon are all that puncture the darkness. The color of everything is gray and silver. Then the sun begins to rise. It is as if God is saying, "Let there be light."

The darkness turns into golden rosiness, and the golden rosiness turns into illuminating rays of light. The color you then see all around you is green, the color of summer, the color of the morning, the color of the trees outside Nazareth where Jesus went each morning to pray and meditate.

Green is the color of Go. When you drive through a small town at night, if you keep the right speed, all the lights are green. If you are going down the road of life at the right speed, all the lights are green. Everything is Yes.

"For the Son of God, Jesus Christ … was not 'Yes' and 'No,' but in him it has always been 'Yes.' For no matter how many promises God has made, they are 'Yes' in Christ" (2 Cor. 1:19–20, NIV).

Green is the color of beginning and of beginning again. It is the color of spring.

Green is the color of growth. Growth is like the passage of days, like the passage of seasons, like the passage of planets in their orbits—without haste, without delay. It is the work of a lifetime. It is both active and restful. Green is the color of growing in the grace and knowledge of our Lord and Savior Jesus Christ.

Green is the color of promise. At the very tip of each small oak branch is a tiny gray bud. The green leaves will turn golden brown in autumn and fall from the trees. The trees will then sleep through the long winter. Encased within each small gray bud, however, is the greenness that is the promise of next spring.

Green is the color of not knowing. When you move to a new place, when you take a new job, you are green. When students first come to a new campus, they are green. They may not even know where to go when they first arrive. They can't get used to which door is unlocked when. And whether to take food off the tray or not. And what to do with the dishes afterward. And when is breakfast? Green is not knowing the names of people around them.

Too easily, we lose our greenness. Too readily, we take on a blasé attitude of knowing everything. It is then we are no longer in a frame of mind to learn. No longer teachable. No longer able to meditate. No longer able to hear the still, small voice of the Holy Spirit. No longer green, we become like the dead stick that cannot bend. We become set in our ways and cannot change without being broken. If a green tomato is plucked from the vine too soon, it will rot. It needs to stay green on the vine a good while before it will ripen properly.

When God said, let there be light, let there be colors, let there be green, nothing could stop His command. But He does not command the words of our mouth and the meditation of our heart to be acceptable. He is a gentleman. It was He who first thought of free will. When we desire that our words be acceptable, however, when we hunger and thirst after righteousness, when we invite Him, by saying, "Let the words of my mouth and the meditation of my heart be acceptable in Your sight" (Ps. 19:14. NKJV), then the Power who created the light brings morning to our lives, brings Go and Yes, brings new beginnings and growth, brings promise, brings learning and changing, brings eternal greenness.

# *Meditation on Orange*

*Time for the
World's Harvest*

Is an orange named after the color? Or is the color named after the fruit? Do we know which came first, the fruit orange or the color orange?

Orange is a strange color. It does not have any rhyme words. Other colors do. Red, fed, head. Yellow, fellow, mellow. Green, bean, lean. Blue, true, zoo. Brown, down, town. Black, jack, sack. White, might, light. There are more than 600,000 words in the English language, but not a single one rhymes with orange.

Orange is on the fence. It is neither red nor yellow. It is halfway between. It wasn't even considered to be a color by the ancients. No orange color is mentioned in the Bible. No orange appears in the list of colors used in the tabernacle. No orange appears in the list of colors used to describe the New Jerusalem. Other colors are mentioned in the Bible, some of them frequently—blue, scarlet, crimson, red, yellow, white, black, green, purple, but no orange. The reason is that the ancient Hebrews never thought of it as a color. There was no word in their language for orange. If something were reddish-orange, they thought of it as red or crimson. If something were yellowish-orange, they thought of it as yellow. If something were exactly in the middle, they could think of it either way. The concept of orange did not exist.

Even in English, there was no thought of orange as a color until the sixteenth century. The first record of its appearing in writing as a color, according to *The Oxford English Dictionary,* was in 1542. Mention was made then of an "orange hue," that is, the hue, or color, of the fruit called an orange. Here is a case where we know which came first.

Orange straddles the fence. It is partly red. It is partly yellow. And can't quite make up its mind. That is why it is a restless color. When we have difficulty making a decision, we are restless, like the color orange. Our lives don't rhyme. We are out of harmony.

*No orange color is mentioned in the Bible.*

Jesus said, "No one can serve two masters; for either he will hate the one and love the other, or else he will be loyal to the one and despise the other. You cannot serve God and mammon" (Matt. 6:24 NKJV).

Jesus also said, "If any man would come after me, let him deny himself and take up his cross and follow me. For whoever would save his life will lose it; and whoever loses his life for my sake and the gospel's will save it. For what does it profit a man, to gain the whole world and forfeit his life? For what can a man give in return for his life? For whoever is ashamed of me and of my words in this adulterous and sinful generation, of him will the Son of man also be ashamed, when he comes in the glory of his Father with the holy angels" (Mark 8:34–38, RSV).

Orange is the color of harvest—the color of pumpkins, persimmons, mangoes, tangerines; the color of the flesh of autumn squashes—Hubbard, acorn, butternut. It is the color of the "harvest moon" that comes in late fall when we realize that summer is over and gone.

Now is the time for the world's harvest. It is an orange time. A restless time. A time to make decisions. A time to get ready. A time to stay ready so that we will not have to say, "The harvest is past, the summer is ended, and we are not saved" (Jer. 8:20).

# *Meditation on Blue*

*May cords of blue*
*Be in the corners*
*of your mind.*

Blue must be a good color. The best entries at the fair get blue ribbons. Those friends we can trust completely are said to be true-blue. The Lord instructed Moses and the children of Israel to use blue in the hangings of the sanctuary. He instructed Solomon to use blue in the hangings of the temple. He directed that the robe of the high priest be blue.

    The Lord even instructed all the Jews of old to wear cords of blue. Even to this day, devout orthodox Jews wear blue on the corners of their garments. Jesus, a devout Jew, wore the blue. If He had not, He would have heard from the Pharisees. The woman who was sick for twelve years reached out to touch the hem of His garment. What was she reaching for, but the blue cords woven into the edge of His robe?

    What is so significant about blue? Why did the Lord choose blue as a symbol of obedience, as a symbol of dedication, of righteousness, of holiness?

    Modern research suggests an answer. Psychologists have discovered that we associate definite feelings and states of mind with specific colors, that we react subconsciously but strongly to colors, and that we are powerfully affected by them. A detergent manufacturer discovered that detergent powder with red or yellow granules won't sell well but that detergent powder with blue granules will. Evidently, we associate cleanliness with blue. We also associate sweetness with blue. A sugar manufacturer discovered that sugar cannot be sold well in red or green packages. Blue needs to be emphasized in the packaging. Psychologists have discovered that emotionally-disturbed people and other sick people are made worse in rooms painted with bright colors but do better in rooms painted blue.

Blue is the color of loyalty, unity, and the sense of belonging.

Blue is purity. It is clear and clean, like water. It is the color of truth, trust, love, dedication, devotion.

Blue is the color of lasting values. It symbolizes holiness to the Lord.

Blue is healing, endurance, empathy.

It is the color of forgiveness, righteousness, salvation.

Blue is contentment, fulfillment, tranquility. It is the sky without a cloud, the calm of an untroubled sea.

Blue is a deep color. It is deep like the heavens, which go on and on and on forever into eternity.

Blue is the color of distant mountains—a symbol of rest, a symbol of victory.

Think blue as you read this text from Isaiah: "The work of righteousness will be peace, And the effect of righteousness, quietness and assurance forever. My people will dwell in a peaceful habitation, In secure dwellings, and in quiet resting places" (Isa. 32:17–18, NKJV).

Think blue as you contemplate Jesus' invitation: "Come to Me, all you who labor and are heavy laden, and I will give you rest. Take My yoke upon you and learn from Me, for I am gentle and lowly in heart, and you will find rest for your souls. For My yoke is easy and My burden is light" (Matt. 11:28–30, NKJV).

As you prepare for the eternal Sabbath, may you experience the peace and contentment that comes from following Jesus. May cords of blue be in the corners of your mind.

## *Worship and the Fine Arts*

*Christian art helps us become
more like Jesus in our attitudes
toward sin and sinners.*

Seventeen years after his *Origin of Species* was published, Charles Darwin wrote this sad confession in his autobiography: "Up to the age of thirty, or beyond it, poetry of many kinds, such as the works of Milton, Gray, Byron, Wordsworth, Coleridge, and Shelley, gave me great pleasure … Formerly pictures gave me considerable, and music very great delight. But now for many years I cannot endure to read a line of poetry … I have also almost lost any taste for pictures or music … My mind seems to have become a kind of machine for grinding general laws out of large collections of facts, but why this should have caused the atrophy of that part of the brain alone, on which the higher tastes depend, I cannot conceive. … If I had to live my life again I would have made a rule to read some poetry and listen to some music at least once every week; for perhaps the parts of my brain now atrophied could thus have been kept active through use. The loss of these tastes is a loss of happiness, and may possibly be injurious to the intellect, and more probably to the moral character, by enfeebling the emotional part of our nature."[7]

If unlike Darwin, you have not allowed your imaginative powers to atrophy, if instead, you have educated your imagination through the enjoyment of poetry, or of music, or of painting, or of one or all of the fine arts, then you have been able, when you assemble with a group of believers on Sabbath morning, to worship God in spirit and in truth, in the beauty of wholeness and holiness.

Through what George Bernard Shaw calls "the power to imagine things as they are without actually seeing them,"[8] you have been able to discern in the imperfect people around you children of the King of the universe. You have been able to perceive the robes of righteousness with which He has clothed them. You have been able to discern the strong ties that bind you to every one of them. You have been able to realize that angels of God are in that place. You have been able to accept the reality of Christ's presence, knowing that where two or three are gathered in His name, He is indeed in the midst of them.

At such times a holy awe has come over you, and you have become no longer part of an audience gathered only to see and hear what goes on up front, but as a member of the congregation of the righteous, you have recognized God as your audience. Through the music and the words of the hymns and anthems and through the poetry of the psalms, you have joined with all creation in giving God your praise.

You have brought an offering, including yourself, and have come into His courts. You have become a watcher and a holy one. You have lifted up your eyes—all your senses—and have entered into the highest experience human beings are privileged to share—the experience of worshiping their Creator.

Your worship need not end at the close of the Sabbath morning worship service. The fine arts can have a part in helping you experience the joy of worship throughout the week. We worship God not only when we come together to ascribe praise to Him, we worship Him when we enjoy His creation, and when we show love to His children.

After all, God created sights, sounds, smells, flavors, and textures for us to enjoy. And He created in us senses with which to enjoy them. In two ways we can express gratitude to God for these His gifts: tell Him our thanks during both private devotions and corporate worship, and show

---

[7] *The Autobiography of Charles Darwin* (Toronto: Collins, 1876, 1958), pp. 138, 139.
[8] George Bernard Shaw, "The Realistic Imagination," in *Listen to Love: Reflections on the Seasons of the Year,* edited by Louis M. Savary et al. (New York: Regina Press, 1969), p. 300.

Him our thanks by enjoying these gifts to the full. We are never out of His presence. Enjoying the things He has made in full knowledge that He sees us enjoy them is worship.

"Your enjoyment of the world is never right," wrote Thomas Traherne, a seventeenth-century English poet, "till every morning you awake in heaven, see yourself in your Father's palace, and look upon the skies and the earth and the air as celestial joys ... You never enjoy the world aright till the sea itself floweth in your veins, till you are clothed with the heavens and crowned with the stars; ... Till you can sing and rejoice and delight in God, as misers do in gold and kings in scepters, you can never enjoy the world."[9]

Most of us are asleep. Having eyes, we see not; having ears, we hear not. Let us thank God for "all builders, poets, painters, and makers of music," for "they open our blind eyes and unstop our deaf ears to the beauty" in God's world."[10] And in doing so, help us enjoy. In helping us enjoy, they help us worship.

We are full of wonder at the changing seasons. But so much of what we see in the seasons of the year we have been educated to discern by the works of artists: the promise of rebirth and resurrection in spring, the growth and freedom of summer, the mature lushness of autumn, and the rare combination of expectation and celebration of winter. Not that the artists have added things to the seasons that are not there. They have simply pointed out things we may not have seen.

It is difficult to take any of the seasons for granted after reading this passage from John Donne, dean of St. Paul's Cathedral when James I was king:

> God made sun and moon to distinguish seasons,
> and day and night,
> and we cannot have the fruits of the earth
> but in their seasons;
> but God hath made no decree to distinguish the seasons
> of his mercies;
> in paradise the fruits were ripe the first minute,
> and in heaven it is always autumn,
> his mercies are ever at their maturity.
> God never says, you should have come yesterday;
> he never says, you must come again tomorrow,

---

[9] Thomas Traherne, *Centuries, Poems, and Thanksgivings,* H.M. Margoliouth, ed. (Oxford: Clarendon Press, 1958), Vol. 1, pp. 14, 15. Spelling and punctuation modernized here.
[10] John Oliver Nelson, ed. *The Student Prayerbook* (New York: Association Press, 1954), p. 112.

but today, if you will hear his voice,
today he will hear you.
He brought light out of darkness,
not out of lesser light;
he can bring thy summer out of winter,
though thou have no spring.
All occasions invite his mercies,
and all times are his seasons.[11]

For having listened to Vivaldi's *The Four Seasons*, for having sung "Fairest Lord Jesus" and "All Things Bright and Beautiful," for having read the chapter on the arrival of spring in Henry David Thoreau's *Walden*, for having viewed a gallery of Monet's paintings of water lilies and haystacks, for having read Robert Frost's "The Path Not Taken" and "Stopping by Woods on a Snowy Evening," we can enjoy the seasons and in that enjoyment worship God.

The artist can do more, however, than unveil the beauties of nature. He can also show us "the sadness and sweetness of humanity to which our selfishness has made us blind." These "masters of form and color and sound" have "power to unlock for us the vaster spaces of emotion and lead us by their hand into the reaches of nobler passion."[12]

> *Jesus loved the sinner, while He hated the sin. We fallen humans tend to do the opposite. We hate the sinner while loving the sin.*

Jesus loved the sinner, while He hated the sin.[13] We fallen humans tend to do the opposite. We hate the sinner while loving the sin. Art often concerns itself with sin and sinners. It may deal with the ugly, the tragic, the frustrating, the sinful. It may be a lamentation rather than a celebration. But good art—Christian art—helps us become more like Jesus in our attitudes toward sin and sinners. It helps us love the sinner while we work to avert evil. Good art is that which treats the human condition in such a way as to arouse compassion.

As our love for others increases and as our perception of their needs is heightened, our aroused feelings will find expression in loving deeds.

---

[11] Quoted in *Listen to Love: Reflections on the Seasons of the Year*, edited by Louis M. Savary, et al. (New York: Regina Press, 1969) p. 347.

[12] Nelson, *op. cit.*, p. 113.

[13] Ellen G. White, *The Desire of Ages*, (Mountain View, CA: Pacific Press Publishing Association, 1898), p. 462.

Through these deeds we glorify God. We worship.
In the hymn, we sing this refrain:

> This world is full of beauty;
> That points the soul above.
> And if we did our duty
> It might be full of love.[14]

Good art is ever telling us this. It is ever educating our perceptions so that we can better see the beauty in the world and the needs of those around us. It is calling on us to enjoy, to love, to worship.

---

[14] G. Massey, "There Lives a Voice Within Me," *The Church Hymnal* (Washington, D.C.: Review and Herald Pub. Assn., 1941), No. 281.

## *Situation for Delight*

**We could call the Sabbath a delight
and take delight in the Lord.**

> *"If you turn back your foot from the sabbath,*
> *from doing your business on my holy day,*
> *and call the sabbath a delight and the holy day*
> *of the LORD honorable;*
> *if you honor it, not going your own ways,*
> *or pursuing your own business,*
> *or talking idly;*
> *then you shall take delight in the LORD,*
> *and I will make you ride upon*
> *the heights of the earth."*[15]

---

[15] Isaiah 58:13, 14. R.S.V., margin.

If I lived at the right place, if I were in the right situation, I would call the Sabbath a delight. I would take delight in the Lord.

On Friday afternoon before sundown, I would have all my chores done, and errands run, and preparations completed. I would welcome the Sabbath as the sun goes down. I would call the Sabbath a delight. I would take delight in the Lord.

On Friday night in summer, I would go to bed rather early. I would relish the softness and smell of clean sheets. I would enjoy the sweetness of rest. I would rest in full assurance that my sins had been forgiven. I would be at peace with God and everyone. I would call the Sabbath a delight. I would take delight in the Lord.

On Sabbath morning, I would be able to wake when the birds begin singing outside my window. I would rise shortly and join them before the traffic inside and outside the house had become too congested. I would put on boots to shield me from the dew, and I would find a woodsy place or a meadow to walk in. I would take pleasure in every flower, in every creature, in every bird's song. I would remember the Creator. I would remember Eden. I would look forward to Eden restored. I would call the Sabbath a delight. I would take delight in the Lord.

In winter, I would not go to bed early on Friday night. Instead, I might take a long walk with a friend around the neighborhood. I would enjoy the quietness of a winter's evening and sometimes the sparkle of moonlight on new-fallen snow. Then I would not rise quite so early the next morning. I would linger in the warmth of blankets. I would call the Sabbath a delight. I would take delight in the Lord.

For breakfast I would always have something special—a Danish roll and perhaps a dish of fresh orange sections cut up with fresh grapefruit. In season, perhaps, a dish of blueberries mixed with red raspberries. A touch of powdered sugar would make it patriotic—red, white, and blue. I would not rush breakfast. No need to dash off to a seven-thirty appointment. I would so relish each bite that my enjoyment would be a prayer of gratitude to God for taste buds and for good things to taste. I would call the Sabbath a delight. I would take delight in the Lord.

I would be on time for Sabbath school, join in the singing, join in the discussion, and enjoy participating with others, knowing that there were those in the group who were sincerely seeking to know truth, to know what is right, who wanted to pattern their lives after God's will. I would take pleasure in being part of such a group. I would call the Sabbath a delight. I would take delight in the Lord.

At church I would not be a spectator. I would consider God to be the audience, the ministers and musicians to be directors of the meeting, and myself to be one of the participants putting on a program FOR God. I would sing my best, for my singing would be directed to the Lord. I would direct my prayers, my meditations, my praise, and my supplications to Him. I would be still in His presence and know that He is God. I would call the Sabbath a delight. I would take delight in the Lord.

I would eat my Sabbath meal with deliberate enjoyment and in the awareness that "the cross of Calvary is stamped on every loaf" and that "every meal [is] a sacrament."[16]

In the afternoon, I might do several things:

I might take our dulcimer from the wall and play and sing "Amazing Grace," "Come, Thou Fount of Every Blessing," "Jesus, Lover of My Soul," and "Simple Gifts"—the only four hymns I know how to play on the dulcimer.

I might listen to religious CDs—all kinds, from the grand baroque music of Vivaldi or the Gabriellis to contemporary folk hymns sung to the accompaniment of a guitar.

I would spend some time reading the Bible. I would read a psalm, then a chapter from the Old Testament, then a psalm, then a chapter from the New Testament, and then a psalm, and so on, thus finding a way to motivate myself through the drier chapters of the Pentateuch and the Chronicles.

I might visit some friends. I would appreciate the wisdom I could gain from those who have lived through many experiences that I have not had. Are we not all epistles from Jesus to each other?

I might go to a museum such as the natural history museum at Harvard University or the Gardner Art Museum in nearby Boston with all its Renaissance religious paintings and the courtyard that is always filled with flowers in blossom.

I might take Helen to a park or wildlife sanctuary such as Drumlin Farm or Great Meadows.

We might go to St. Joseph's Abbey in Spenser to hear the monks sing Gregorian chants during vespers.

There are so many things I might do. And most of them I would do with Helen. We would call the Sabbath a delight. We would take delight in the Lord.

---

[16] Ellen G. White, *The Desire of Ages*, (Mountain View, CA: Pacific Press Publishing Association, 1898), p. 680.

As the Sabbath ended, I would renew my covenant with God. I would begin the new week in harmony with Him, who is all love and goodness, who gave us the gift of the Sabbath, who gave us the gift of His Son. I would call the Sabbath a delight. I would take delight in the Lord.

I would do these things if I lived at the right place, if I were in the right situation.

Ah, but I am! and so are all of us.

If we only would, we could call the Sabbath a delight. We could take delight in the Lord. We could say, "I delight to do Your will, O my God, And Your law is within my heart" (Ps. 40:8, NKJV).

# The Freeing of Long Pond

*Lord, Breathe upon Me*
*gentle or violent winds—*
*but Warm.*

*(Long Pond is a small lake hidden away in a thickly-forested township in north-central Massachusetts, not far from the New Hampshire line. Except for a primitive cabin, the nearest habitation is a mile away. Whenever I went there, I wrote in my Long Pond Journal. Here are some selections.)*

**January 12.**

"Praise the LORD, O Jerusalem; praise thy God, O Zion. …. He giveth snow like wool: he scattereth the hoarfrost like ashes. He casteth forth his ice like morsels: who can stand before his cold? He sendeth out his word, and melteth them: he causeth his wind to blow, and the waters flow" (Ps. 147:12, 16–18).

Nearly everything in its solid state is heavier than in its liquid state. Water is an exception: ice floats. It is floating now on Long Pond. Sixteen inches thick!

Whoever made snow and ice is far greater than I.
Whoever made evening and morning,
darkness and light,
skies and lakes,
grass and trees is far greater than I.
Whoever made fish and fowl,
creeping things and crawling things,
Whoever made summer and winter,
Whoever made snow and ice is
far greater than I.
Like rivers and ponds, I praise God and
magnify Him forever.
Like clear water and dark water,
Like beaver and muskrat,
Like pickerel and trout,
Like herons and warblers,
Like mergansers and mallards, I praise
God and magnify Him forever.
Like reflections and ripples,
Like lily pads and maple leaves,
Like crackling sounds and snapping sounds,
swishing sounds and howling sounds,
I praise God and magnify Him forever,
Like wind and rain,
Like mist and fog,
Like snow and ice, I praise God
and magnify Him forever.

**February 8**

Even if I knew I were to sleep the second death and never wake up, I would still love and praise the Lord, for He is working all things together for good. The creation is longing for the time when all will be harmony and love, for the time when God will finish making it turn out right.

Even if the sun were to blow up and its particles were scattered over millions of light-years of space, all will still be right—all will eventually work together for good. Therefore, I praise God. I honor Him. I thank Him for His goodness. I love Him.

Even if I were to turn away from Him and be lost, He would never forget me. For eons of eternity, He would think of me with joy—and pain.

Joy that I praised Him and loved Him once, that I was once grateful for what He had done for me. Pain that I somehow turned away from Him.

Always He will be conscious of me: my name is graven on the palms of His hands. How can I not love Him with all my mind, my strength, my body, my soul? How could I turn from Him?

O Jesus, I desire Your salvation. I always want to be in Your presence. But even if I knew now that I would be lost in eternal sleep, I love You, for You will make all things turn out right. You will cause the ice to melt and the waters to flow.

*Even if I were to turn away from Him and be lost, He would never forget me.*

**March 2.**

> God of the night and God of the morning,
> Thank You for waking me up to all these Your blessings.
> For the warmth of the stove here in the cabin,
> For the brightness of the sky,
> For snow,
> For snow melting early,
> For teaberry leaves green throughout winter,
> For trailing arbutus getting ready to bloom,
> For the smell of white-pine resin on my hands from fire logs,
> For fire logs of great variety—oak, maple, birch, pine, hemlock,
> For thousands of trees still standing,
> For ice on the pond,
> For water beneath the ice,
> For the lily branches on the bottom of the pond,
> For the fish that swim among the lilies,
> For the beaver lodge at the edge of the pond,
> For beaver stumps on the shore,
> For the expansion and contraction of the stove
>     as the fire flares up and then dies down,
> For the expansion and contraction of timbers in the cabin,
> For the drip-drip-drip of water from the snow melting on the roof,
> For the March wind—gentle now,
> For the stronger March wind yet to come,
> For the chickadee singing outside the window,
> For the smell of food cooking,

For the smell of the wood burned and the food cooked in this cabin
   during its sixty years,
For the smell of sweetened red coal oil in the desk lamp,
For the peace of being alone with You,
Jesus—more than a mile from the closest human habitation,
For knowing that there are, nevertheless,
other humans not too far away—
I hear cars driving up Jacob's Hill Road,
I hear a plane overhead,
I hear a train in the distance—
For Helen to go home to,
For You, Jesus, who broods over all,
I give You thanks.

**March 23.**

Long Pond is still frozen over. To all appearances, it is dead. It has closed its eye to the surrounding hills and the sky above it. The pond does not move. It has no waves—no ripples when the wind blows. It does not shimmer in the moonlight. No lily pads undulate with its motion. Young bluegills with their iridescent blue do not swim slowly to the surface. Canada geese migrating north choose elsewhere to stop. Beaver are quiet in their lodges, waiting for the thaw when they can resume their quest for poplar twigs.

When the ice first came, it formed at the edge of the pond—thin ice that was crystalline and brittle. Like a contemporary abstract sculpture, it was a thing of beauty in and of itself. At the beginning of November, early one morning, I came to the pond for an adventure—to see the dawn come in. I had arisen at 3:00 a.m. and was in the canoe long before sunrise. Shortly, the moon set. Everything disappeared in the darkness. But I could hear the thin ice at the edge of the pond cracking from the waves set in motion by my paddling.

The first big freeze of the season came November 7. Four mornings later, I was at the pond again and found about a quarter-inch of ice covering all but a small section in the middle of the pond. The ice completely disappeared during the day but reformed during the following night. Then, as the days went by, the water became gradually colder. And so did the air. By November 17, thin patches of ice remained on the pond throughout the day, but not enough to prevent canoeing. The pond continued like this through the middle of December. Sometime in late December or early January, the pond finally became locked in for the winter. On January 12, the ice was sixteen inches thick.

A pond, I suppose, can be freed in two ways. One way is gentle. The weather gets warmer gradually, causing the ice to melt gradually. Then, one morning, there is nothing but a few patches of thin ice. A few hours later, the ice is gone. Ripples shimmer in the sunlight, and water lily buds from below begin responding to the sun.

Another way is through violence. If a heavy rain followed by a heavy wind comes when the ice is at the right stage of sponginess, the warm water flowing under and over the ice can cause it to crack into large slabs, which the wind piles together in clumps. The waves stir the slabs and water together, melting some and forcing others onto the bank. And the pond becomes unlocked.

I came up this weekend to see the pond get free. Maybe I will get to see it happen, and maybe I won't. Its appearance changes every hour. A heavy rain came yesterday. Today has been warm, sunny, and windy. During the day, water from the upper channel and from the melting surface has swept across the ice. I can hear the lapping of water against the opposite shore. The wind is blowing that way. And the ice is free from the shore. One giant cake of ice is floating over the forty acres of pond. The pond is pulsating. It is waking up. Streams are forming throughout this giant cake of ice, cutting their way through. Will the cake of ice break up into smaller chunks tonight? Will the wind increase and throw slabs of ice onto the opposite shore?

**April 6.**

While I was away, the miracle came. Whether gently or violently, I do not know. All I know is that two weeks ago, Long Pond was frozen over. Today the ice is gone. Perhaps I was the first to put a canoe on the pond after the long winter. As I paddled toward the beaver lodge, I saw, a hundred feet ahead of me, gracefully swimming on the shimmering water, a large Canada goose, which looked straight at me as she floated near the water shrubs. I stopped my rowing. She flew up almost immediately and headed north over the marsh, honking all the way. The water was crystal clear. I could see the buds of water lilies pushing up from the sandy bottom. The entrance to the beaver lodge, an opening the size of a large watermelon, was clearly visible a few feet below the surface. Nearby a young beaver sat in the sun grooming itself. A flock of red-winged blackbirds flew over, looking for nesting ground at the edge of the pond. A flock of mallards followed, heading for the marsh by the Tully River north of the pond.

*The ice is gone. Long Pond is free.*

It seems to me, Jesus, sometimes I am like a frozen pond—cold, unfeeling, and unfruitful. Yet underneath my silent surface is the life You put there. Breathe upon me gentle or violent winds—but warm.

Amen.

*"Praise the Lord, O Jerusalem; praise thy God, O Zion. ... He giveth snow like wool: he scattereth the hoarfrost like ashes. He casteth forth his ice like morsels: who can stand before his cold? He sendeth out his word, and melteth them: he causeth his wind to blow, and the waters flow."*

*Yes, Jesus. Yes.*

# *About the Author*

Richard Lynn Sauls was born January 11, 1933, in a peanut-farm cottage thirty miles from Plains, Georgia, and lived in various places in the South until he graduated from Fayetteville, North Carolina, High School.

He earned a bachelor of arts in religion from Southern Missionary College (now Southern Adventist University), a master of arts in English from Vanderbilt University, a Ph.D. in English from the University of Iowa, and completed post-graduate work in journalism at Boston University.

Lynn is a member of the College Seventh-day Adventist Church in South Lancaster, Massachusetts, has been an active member of the Adventist Church since his senior year in high school, has served as elder, has spoken in many churches, and has written many published articles, devotions, and poems, receiving several top awards from the Associated Church Press.

He had a forty-three-year career in education, first serving as an elementary and secondary teacher and principal before teaching literature, creative writing, and journalism at several colleges and universities, including Atlantic Union College, Andrews University, and Southern Adventist University. He was writing teacher of many writers and editors, including columnist and book-writer Andy Nash and editor of *Adventist Review* Bill Knott.

Recently, Lynn said the five best things that happened to him are giving his heart to Jesus when he was twelve years old, accepting the Adventist message when he was seventeen, attending Southern Missionary College, enjoying a sixty-seven-year marriage with Helen, and seeing their son grow up to make them proud.

Lynn enjoyed watching beavers on Long Pond in Royalston, Massachusetts, swimming in the Gulf of Mexico at Naples, Florida, and reading books and traveling with his wife Helen. Recently, he has enjoyed time with his family; associating with former colleagues and students, and with friends at the Gables of Fitchburg, Massachusetts; and putting together this book. He hopes you will be blessed by reading it.

# *Bibliography*

Eisenberg, Lawrence. "Who Would You Most Like to Interview—And What Would You Ask?" *Good Housekeeping*, October 1986.

Danoff, Bill, Taffy Nivert, and John Denver. "Take Me Home, Country Roads." Copyright 1971, Cherry Lane Music Co. Used by permission. All rights reserved.

Darwin, Charles. *The Autobiography of Charles Darwin.* Toronto: Collins, 1876, 1958.

Franklin, Benjamin. *Autobiography of Benjamin Franklin*, ed. John Bigelow. Philadelphia, PA: J. B. Lippincott & Co., 1868.

Kendig, Frank and Richard Hutton. *Life Spans: Or How Long Things Last.* New York: Holt, Rinehart and Winston, 1980.

Massey, G. "There Lives a Voice Within Me," *The Church Hymnal.* Washington, DC: Review and Herald Publishing Association, 1941.

Nelson, John Oliver, ed. *The Student Prayerbook.* New York, NY: Association Press, 1954.

Savary, Louis M., et al. *Listen to Love: Reflections on the Seasons of the Year*. New York: Regina Press, 1969.

Traherne, Thomas, *Centuries, Poems, and Thanksgivings,* Vol. 1. H.M. Margoliouth, ed. Oxford: Clarendon Press, 1958.

White, Ellen G. *The Desire of Ages.* Mountain View, CA: Pacific Press Publishing Association, 1898.

## TEACH Services, Inc.
P U B L I S H I N G

We invite you to view the complete
selection of titles we publish at:
**www.TEACHServices.com**

We encourage you to write us
with your thoughts about this,
or any other book we publish at:
**info@TEACHServices.com**

TEACH Services' titles may be purchased in
bulk quantities for educational, fund-raising,
business, or promotional use.
**bulksales@TEACHServices.com**

Finally, if you are interested in seeing
your own book in print, please contact us at:
**publishing@TEACHServices.com**

We are happy to review your manuscript at no charge.

www.ingramcontent.com/pod-product-compliance
Lightning Source LLC
Chambersburg PA
CBHW042133160426
43199CB00021B/2897